GREAT
GIANT
CRANES

BY NATALIE HUMPHREY

Gareth Stevens
PUBLISHING

Please visit our website, www.garethstevens.com. For a free color catalog of all our high-quality books, call toll free 1-800-542-2595 or fax 1-877-542-2596.

Portions of this work were originally authored by Kenny Allen and published as *Giant Cranes*. All new material in this edition is authored by Natalie Humphrey.

Cataloging-in-Publication Data

Names: Humphrey, Natalie.
Title: Great giant cranes / Natalie Humphrey.
Description: New York : Gareth Stevens Publishing, 2023. | Series: Mega machines! | Includes glossary and index.
Identifiers: ISBN 9781538283035 (pbk.) | ISBN 9781538283059 (library bound) | ISBN 9781538283066 (ebook)
Subjects: LCSH: Cranes, derricks, etc.–Juvenile literature.
Classification: LCC TJ1363.H86 2023 | DDC 621.873–dc23

Published in 2023 by
Gareth Stevens Publishing
2455 Clinton Street
Buffalo, NY 14224

Copyright © 2023 Gareth Stevens Publishing

Designer: Deanna Paternostro
Editor: Natalie Humphrey

Photo credits: Cover, p. 1 bon9/Shutterstock.com; pp. 3, 4, 6, 8, 10, 12, 14, 16, 18, 20, 21 (bottom), 22, 23, 24 Nataliia K/Shutterstock.com; p. 5 AMatveev/Shutterstock.com; p. 7 Dmitry-Arhangel 29/Shutterstock.com; p. 9 Quality Stock Arts/Shutterstock.com; p. 11 KPhrom/Shutterstock.com; p. 13 SergeyKlopotov/Shutterstock.com; p. 15 Kondrelena/Shutterstock.com; p. 17 Evgeniy Kurochkin/Shutterstock.com; p. 19 potowizard/Shutterstock.com; p. 21 (top) Robert Timoney/Alamy Stock Photo.

CPSIA compliance information: Batch #CWGS23: For further information contact Gareth Steven at 1-800-542-2595.

Find us on

CONTENTS

Boldface words appear in the glossary.

Mega Cranes

Some jobs are too heavy for people to do on their own. Cranes are mega machines used to help people move loads from place to place. Cranes can be found on farms, at **construction** sites, and they can even be found on the back of trucks!

Parts of a Crane

When you see a crane, the first thing you likely notice is the long arm stretching into the sky. This is the boom. Many cranes also have a jib that reaches out over the ground. This makes it easier for the crane to lift a load.

Lifting Wonders

To lift something, cranes use a **pulley system**. Some cranes have a heavy **hook** to carry loads. The hook is fixed to a long rope or cable. The hook is used to hold onto heavy loads. Wheels in the pulleys allow the rope to move smoothly.

PULLEY

PULLEY

Hooks on Ropes

A crane's rope is attached to a **hoist**. The rope is wrapped around the hoist on a part called a drum. The hoist spins the drum to let out rope. To lift something, the hoist spins the other way and winds the rope around the drum.

HOIST

DRUM

11

Tough Towers

When workers are building a **skyscraper**, they may use a tower crane. Tower cranes have long **masts**. They also have jibs to lift heavy loads. When workers need to reach higher, they can add another piece to the crane's mast!

Truck-Mounted Cranes

Some cranes are built to move from place to place. These cranes are **mounted** to the back of trucks. Tow-truck cranes are small. However, some truck-mounted cranes are giant. The tallest truck-mounted cranes can lift loads 47 stories into the sky!

Cranes Overhead

Overhead cranes look different than other cranes. They don't have masts or booms. The hoist moves on a board. The beam moves on a set of tracks. The crane can pick up something on one side of a factory and move it to the other side.

A Special Overhead Crane

One type of overhead crane is a gantry crane. Gantry cranes have hoists that move back and forth on a beam. The entire crane moves on wheels or tracks. Gantry cranes lift giant **containers** off ships and put them onto trucks.

SAFETY FIRST

AFETY FIRST

19

The Biggest Cranes

There are many big cranes in the world used for big jobs! The tallest is the Sarens Giant Crane. It's 820 feet (250 m) tall and called "Big Carl." The strongest is the Taisun gantry crane. It can lift 20,133 tons (18,264 mt)!

Mega Machine Facts: Sarens SGC-250 "Big Carl"

Location: Somerset, United Kingdom

Height: 820 feet (250 m)

Number of Engines: 12

Heaviest Weight Lifted: 5,000 tons (4,536 mt)

GLOSSARY

construction: Having to do with the act of building something.

container: An object used to hold something.

hoist: A machine people use to lift loads that are heavy.

hook: A tool that is curved or bent and is used for pulling, holding, or catching something.

mast: A long pole that supports something.

mounted: Attached to something.

pulley system: A wheel or group of wheels that is combined with a rope or chain to lift and lower objects.

skyscraper: A very large, tall building.

BOOKS

Allan, John. *Let's Look at Monster Machines*. Minneapolis, MN: Hungry Tomato, 2019.

Pettiford, Rebecca. *Cranes*. Minneapolis, MN: Jump!, Inc., 2023.

WEBSITES

Kids Britannica
kids.britannica.com/students/article/crane-and-derrick/273846
Learn about cranes and other important construction equipment.

Wonderopolis
wonderopolis.org/wonder/how-does-a-crane-work
Learn more about how cranes work and learn how to build your own crane.

INDEX